BOOK OF BIBLE KNOWLEDGE

Abingdon Press

Book of Bible Knowledge

Copyright © 1987 by Abingdon Press

All rights reserved.

ISBN 0-687-03670-4

All Scripture quotations in this publication are from the Holy Bible, New International Version. Copyright © 1973, 1978, 1984, International Bible Society.

The chart and Biblical Time-Line (adapted) in this book are from *Aids for Teaching the Bible Kit*. © 1983 by Graded Press. Used by permission.

MANUFACTURED BY THE PARTHENON PRESS AT
NASHVILLE, TENNESSEE, UNITED STATES OF AMERICA

Foreword

The Bible is a great source of inspiration as well as the history of our faith. Presented here are facts about the Bible, great passages, suggestions for reading the Scriptures, and other concise information to help you become more familiar with this great Book.

Use this booklet for your own private meditation and study or with a study group. Either way, you will find it a handy guide. The time-line of Bible events and the biblical genealogies are quick references to have available anytime you read your Bible.

Contents

The Sixty-six Books of the Bible	7
Facts About the Bible	9
Key Words of the Books of the Bible	10
Ten Great Passages of the Bible	14
One-Hundred and One Great Chapters of the Bible	19
The Wonderful Christ	23
Biblical Genealogies	24
Great Prayers of the Bible	27
More Great Prayers of the Bible	30
Bible Twos	31
Bible Threes	33
How to Grow	36
Helps for Bible Reading	37
The Bible Story in Two-Hundred and Fifty Words	38
Biblical Time-Line	40
My Favorite Bible Passages	46

The Sixty-six Books of the Bible

OLD TESTAMENT (39 Books)

Law, 5 books

	Chapters
Genesis	50
Exodus	40
Leviticus	27
Numbers	36
Deuteronomy	34

History, 12 books

Joshua	24
Judges	21
Ruth	4
First Samuel	31
Second Samuel	24
First Kings	22
Second Kings	25
First Chronicles	29
Second Chronicles	36
Ezra	10
Nehemiah	13
Esther	10

Poetry, 5 books

Job	42
Psalms	150
Proverbs	31
Ecclesiastes	12
Song of Solomon	8

Major Prophets, 5 books

Isaiah	66
Jeremiah	52
Lamentations	5
Ezekiel	48
Daniel	12

Minor Prophets, 12 books

Hosea	14
Joel	3
Amos	9
Obadiah	1
Jonah	4
Micah	7
Nahum	3
Habakkuk	3
Zephaniah	3
Haggai	2
Zechariah	14
Malachi	4

NEW TESTAMENT (27 Books)

Gospels, 4 books

	Chapters
Matthew	28
Mark	16
Luke	24
John	21

History, 1 book

Acts	28

Epistles, 21 books

	Chapters
Romans	16
First Corinthians	16
Second Corinthians	13
Galatians	6
Ephesians	6
Philippians	4
Colossians	4
First Thessalonians	5
Second Thessalonians	3
First Timothy	6
Second Timothy	4
Titus	3
Philemon	1
Hebrews	13
James	5
First Peter	5
Second Peter	3
First John	5
Second John	1
Third John	1
Jude	1

Prophecy, 1 book

Revelation	22

The Old Testament was written before Jesus was born.

The New Testament was written after Jesus was born, died, arose from the dead, and ascended into heaven.

Facts About the Bible

The word "Bible" comes from the Greek word meaning "books."

The first book printed was the famed Gutenberg Bible, printed in Germany in 1456.

The Bible is the most widely circulated book in the English language.

The Bible is available in over 1,500 languages around the world.

The Bible contains 3,566,480 letters, 773,693 words, 31,102 verses, 1,189 chapters, and 66 books.

The middle verse of the Bible is Psalm 118:8.

The shortest verse of the Bible is John 11:35.

Second Kings 19 and Isaiah 37 are almost alike.

The word Lord occurs 1,855 times.

The New Testament has about 180 direct quotations from the Old Testament.

The New Testament as we know it today was first accepted in A.D. 367.

The King James or Authorized Version of the Bible was first printed in 1611.

Key Words of the Books of the Bible

Genesis—book of beginnings, human failure

Exodus—book of redemption

Leviticus—book of sacrifice and priesthood

Numbers—book of wilderness wanderings

Deuteronomy—book of conduct for Canaan

Joshua—book of faith, conflict, and victory

Judges—book of failure in Canaan

Ruth—book of typical prophecy

I Samuel—royal government in the hands of Saul

II Samuel—royal government in the hands of David

I Kings—royal government of Solomon and his successors

II Kings—royal government in its decline

I Chronicles—God's earthly government connected with the throne and the Ark

II Chronicles—God's earthly government in the House of David

Ezra—ecclesiastical history on return from Babylon

Nehemiah—civil condition on return from Babylon

Esther—God's secret government toward Israel

Job—book of individual discipline for learning of self

Psalms—experimental holy song and messianic prophecy

Proverbs—wisdom for the world

Ecclesiastes—world too small for the human heart

Song of Solomon—one who found the object too great for his heart

Isaiah—comprehensive and magnificent prophecy

Jeremiah—judgments upon Judah, the nations, and the latter-day glory

Lamentations—godly feelings in view of Israel's sorrow

Ezekiel—judgment upon Israel and connected nations with future blessings of Israel

Daniel—Gentile political history

Hosea—Israel's moral condition—past, present, and future

Joel—universal judgment and latter-day blessings

Amos—judgment upon the Gentiles and all Israel, with future restoration of the latter

Obadiah—judgment upon Edom

Jonah—judgment upon Nineveh and its repentance

Micah—judgment and future blessing of Jerusalem and Samaria

Nahum—judgment upon Assyria

Habakkuk—book of Jewish spiritual exercise

Zephaniah—book of unsparing judgment and blessing upon the remnant of Israel

Haggai—encouragement in rebuilding the temple

Zechariah—the "last days" connected with Israel

Malachi—Jehovah's last pleading with Israel

Matthew—son and Lord according to promise

Mark—the Meeter of human need

Luke—the Son of man in his service among people

John—the Son of God in the moral glory of his person and ways

Acts—Christ in heaven and the energy of the Holy Spirit on earth, what Jesus continued to do and teach, how the church was gathered and built, the progress of the kingdom

Romans—Christianity unfolded, righteousness, and way people can be with God

I Corinthians—church order and discipline, our relations to one another in the church

II Corinthians—Christian ministry and superiority over circumstances, our relation to the Word and to them

Galatians—Christian blessing and liberty contrasted in the Law, stand fast in the liberty wherewith Christ has made you free, the Spirit in the beginning, middle, and end of Christian life and power

Ephesians—Christ the measure of Christian standing and blessing; together with Christ

Philippians—Christian experience; perfection that is not perfect; one thing to do

Colossians—the church's glories and fullness in Christ, her head

I Thessalonians—Christ's coming to and for the church, and her eternal blessedness

II Thessalonians—Christ's coming with his saints, the eternal judgment of unbelievers

I Timothy—church order according to God

II Timothy—church disorder and the individual pathway

Titus—Christian qualification for the ministry and godly conduct

Philemon—Christian love, counting on master's love for slave

Hebrews—our apostle's priest, sacrifice, and witness

James—common sense Christianity in and out of the church

I Peter—God's righteous government in relation to saints

II Peter—God's righteous judgment on the public Christian profession

I John—Christ the eternal life and power of communion with God

II John—Christ and the truth, the safeguard against heresy

III John—Christian hospitality to the saints, especially to laborers

Jude—apostasy traced down to the last days

Revelation—Christ assuming the government of the world, things to come

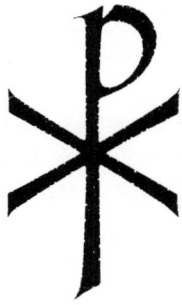

Ten Great Passages of the Bible

Exodus 20:1-17
The Ten Commandments

And God spoke all these words:
"I am the Lord your God, who brought you out of Egypt, out of the land of slavery.
"You shall have no other gods before me.
"You shall not make for yourself an idol in the form of anything in heaven above or on the earth beneath or in the waters below. You shall not bow down to them or worship them; for I, the Lord your God, am a jealous God, punishing the children for the sin of the fathers to the third and fourth generation of those who hate me, but showing love to a thousand generations of those who love me and keep my commandments.
"You shall not misuse the name of the Lord your God, for the Lord will not hold anyone guiltless who misuses his name.
"Remember the Sabbath day by keeping it holy. Six days you shall labor and do all your work, but the seventh day is a Sabbath to the Lord your God. On it you shall not do any work, neither you, nor your son or daughter, nor your manservant or maidservant, nor your animals, nor the alien within your gates. For in six days the Lord made the heavens and the earth, the sea, and all that is in them, but he rested on the seventh day. Therefore the Lord blessed the Sabbath day and made it holy.
"Honor your father and your mother, so that you may live long in the land the Lord your God is giving you.
"You shall not murder.
"You shall not commit adultery.
"You shall not steal.
"You shall not give false testimony againss your neighbor.
"You shall not covet your neighbor's house. You shall not covet your neighbor's wife, or his manservant or maidservant, his ox or donkey, or anything that belongs to your neighbor."

Psalm 23
A psalm of David.

The Lord is my shepherd, I shall not be in want.
    He makes me lie down in green pastures,
he leads me beside quiet waters,
    he restores my soul.
He guides me in paths of righteousness
    for his name's sake.
Even though I walk
    through the valley of the shadow of death,
I will fear no evil,
    for you are with me;
your rod and your staff,
    they comfort me.

You prepare a table before me
    in the presence of my enemies.
You anoint my head with oil;
    my cup overflows.
Surely goodness and love will follow me
    all the days of my life,
and I will dwell in the house of the Lord
    forever.

Psalm 100
A psalm. For giving thanks.

Shout for joy to the Lord, all the earth.
    Worship the Lord with gladness;
    come before him with joyful songs.
Know that the Lord is God.
    It is he who made us, and we are his;
    we are his people, the sheep of his pasture.

Enter his gates with thanksgiving
    and his courts with praise;
    give thanks to him and praise his name.
For the Lord is good and his love endures forever;
    his faithfulness continues through all generations.

Matthew 5:3-10
The Beatitudes

"Blessed are the poor in spirit,
    for theirs is the kingom of heaven.
Blessed are those who mourn,
    for they will be comforted.
Blessed are the meek,
    for they will inherit the earth.
Blessed are those who hunger and thirst for righteousness,
    for they will be filled.
Blessed are the merciful,
    for they will be shown mercy.
Blessed are the pure in heart,
    for they will see God.
Blessed are the peacemakers,
    for they will be called sons of God.
Blessed are those who are persecuted because of righteousness,
    for theirs is the kingdom of heaven."

Matthew 6:9-13
The Lord's Prayer

"This, then, is how you should pray:
'Our Father in heaven,
hallowed be your name,
your kingdom come,
your will be done
    on earth as it is in heaven.
Give us today our daily bread.
Forgive us our debts,
    as we also have forgiven our debtors.
And lead us not into temptation,
but deliver us from the evil one.' "

Matthew 22:37-40
The Greatest Commandment

Jesus replied: " 'Love the Lord your God with all your heart and with all your soul and with all your mind.' This is the first and greatest commandment. And the second is like it: 'Love your neighbor as yourself.' All the Law and the Prophets hang on these two commandments."

Matthew 28:18-20
The Great Commission

Then Jesus came to them and said, "All authority in heaven and on earth has been given to me. Therefore go and make disciples of all nations, baptizing them in the name of the Father and of the Son and of the Holy Spirit, and teaching them to obey everything I have commanded you. And surely I am with you always, to the very end of the age."

John 3:16

"For God so loved the world that he gave his one and only Son, that whoever believes in him shall not perish but have eternal life."

I Corinthians 11:23-26
The Lord's Supper

For I received from the Lord what I also passed on to you: The Lord Jesus, on the night he was betrayed, took bread, and when he had given thanks, he broke it and said, "This is my body, which is for you; do this in remembrance of me." In the same way, after supper he took the cup, saying, "This cup is the new covenant in my blood; do this, whenever you drink it, in remembrance of me." For whenever you eat this bread and drink this cup, you proclaim the Lord's death until he comes.

I Corinthians 13:1-13
Love

If I speak in the tongues of men and of angels, but have not love, I am only a resounding gong or a clanging cymbal. If I have the gift of prophecy, and can fathom all mysteries and all knowledge, and if I have a faith that can move mountains, but have not love, I am nothing. If I give all I possess to the poor and surrender my body to the flames, but have not love, I gain nothing.

Love is patient, love is kind. It does not envy, it does not boast, it is not proud. It is not rude, it is not self-seeking, it is not easily angered, it keeps no record of wrongs. Love does not delight in evil but rejoices in the truth. It always protects, always trusts, always hopes, always preseveres.

Love never fails. But where there are prophecies, they will cease; where there are tongues, they will be stilled; where there is knowledge, it will pass away. For we know in part and we prophesy in part, but when perfection comes, the imperfect disappears. When I was a child, I talked like a child, I thought like a child, I reasoned like a child. When I became a man, I put childish ways behind me. Now we see but a poor reflection as in a mirror; then we shall see face to face. Now I know in part; then I shall know fully, even as I am fully known.

And now these three remain: faith, hope and love. But the greatest of these is love.

One-Hundred and One Great Chapters of the Bible

Abiding	John	15
Annunciation	Luke	1
Ascension	Acts	1
Anti-Christ	II Thessalonians	2
Armor of God	Ephesians	6
Bondage of Sin	Romans	7 ff
Bread of Life	John	6
Brotherly Consideration	Romans	14
Brotherly Love	I John	4
Burden Bearing	Galatians	6
Charity	I Corinthians	13
Chastening	Hebrews	12
Character Building	I Corinthians	3
Christ's Supremacy	Hebrews	1
City of God	Revelation	21
Concentration	Philippians	3
Confidence	Psalm	46
Consecration	Romans	12
Consolation	John	14
Contentment	Philippians	4
Courage	Joshua	1
Creation	Genesis	1
Crucifixion	Matthew	27

See also Mark 15; Luke 23; John 19

Day of Pentecost	Acts	2
Divine Enthronement	Psalm	97
Divine Knowledge	Psalm	139
Divine Revelation	Psalm	19
Election	Romans	9
Encouragement	Psalm	42
Exodus	Exodus	13

Faith	Hebrews	11
Faith and Works	James	2
Fall of Humanity	Genesis	3
Flesh and Spirit	Romans	8
Fool	Proverbs	26
Freedom from Sin	Romans	6
Glorying	II Corinthians	12
Godly Man	Psalm	1
God's House	Psalm	84
God's Mercy	Psalm	136
Good Shepherd	John	10
Good Shepherd	Psalm	23
Grace	Ephesians	2
Greatness of God	Isaiah	40
Heavenly Home	Revelation	22
Holiness	Colossians	3
Holy Spirit	John	16
Humility	Philippians	2
Immortal Life	I Corinthians	15
Instrumental Music	Psalm	149 ff
Invitation	Isaiah	55
Justification	Romans	5
Keeper of Israel	Psalm	121
King of Kings	Psalm	72
Kingdom of Heaven	Matthew	13
Lazarus Called to Life	John	11
Liberty	Galatians	5
Life's Brevity	Psalm	90
Living Water	John	4
Lord's Supper	I Corinthians	11

Also Matthew 26; Mark 14; Luke 22

Lost and Found	Luke	15
Loving-kindness	Psalm	103
Missionary	Psalm	96
Nativity	Luke	2
Old Age	Ecclesiastes	12
Passover	Exodus	12
Paul and Agrippa	Acts	26
Paul's Conversion	Acts	9
Penitent's Prayer	Psalm	51
Peter and Cornelius	Acts	10
Praise	Psalm	148

See also Psalms 146; 147; 149; 150

Prayer of Christ	John	17
Preaching	I Corinthians	2
Proverb	Psalm	37

Refuge and Fortress	Psalm	91
Regeneration	John	3
Rest	Hebrews	4
Resurrection	Luke	24

See also Matthew 28; Mark 16; John 20

Rich Man	Luke	16
Separation	II Corinthians	6
Sermon on the Mount	Matthew	5 ff

See also Luke 6

Service	Luke	10
Seven Churches of Asia	Revelation	2 ff
Signs of the Times	Matthew	24

See also Mark 13; Luke 21

Spiritual Life	I Corinthians	12
Suffering Savior	Isaiah	53
Tempest	Psalm	29
Temporal Supply	Luke	12
Temptation	Matthew	4
Ten Commandments	Exodus	20
Tongue	James	3
Transfiguration	Mark	9

See also Matthew 17; Luke 9

Unity	Ephesians	4
Vigilance	I Thessalonians	5
Watchfulness and Faithfulness	Matthew	25
Wisdom	Proverbs	4
Witness Bearing	John	1
Word of God	Psalm	119
Worship	Psalm	95
Young Men	Proverbs	3
Zion's Glory	Isaiah	60

The Wonderful Christ

The Prayerful Christ—Luke 22:41
The Troubling Christ—Matthew 14:26
The Enthroned Christ—Matthew 25:31
The Borrowing Christ—Mark 11:3
The Confident Christ—Matthew 16:28
The Expectant Christ—Hebrews 10:13
The Enriching Christ—Romans 10:12
The Indignant Christ—John 2:15
The Steadfast Christ—Luke 9:51
The Emotional Christ—Luke 19:41
The Aggressive Christ—Isaiah 59:18-19
The Conquering Christ—Revelation 6:2
The Indwelling Christ—Ephesians 3:17
The Purposeful Christ—John 18:37
The Persistent Christ—Isaiah 42:4
The Triumphant Christ—Luke 24:5
The Unexpected Christ—Luke 24:15
The Optimistic Christ—John 16:20-22
The Sacrificing Christ—I Corinthians 15:3

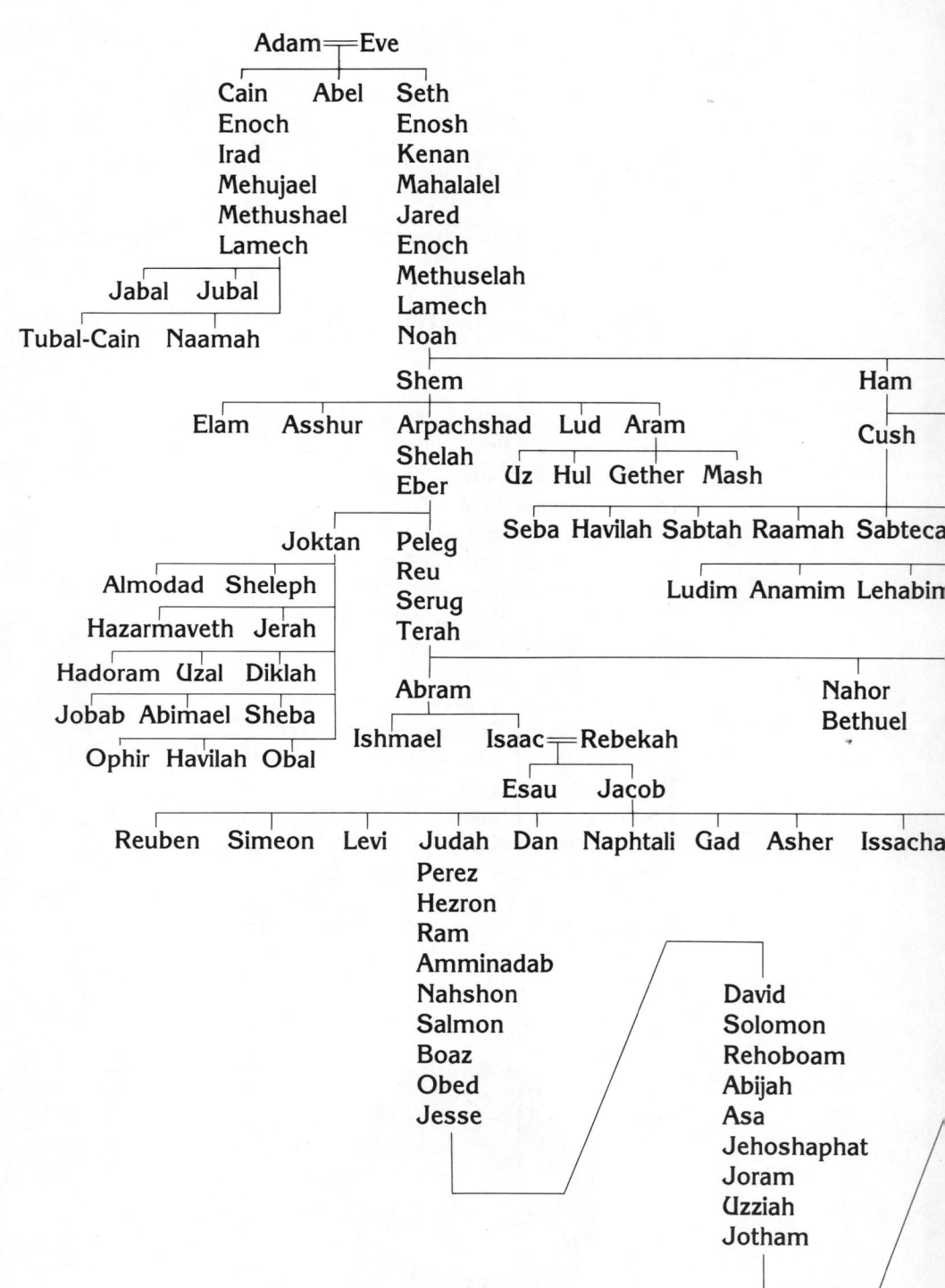

Biblical Genealogies

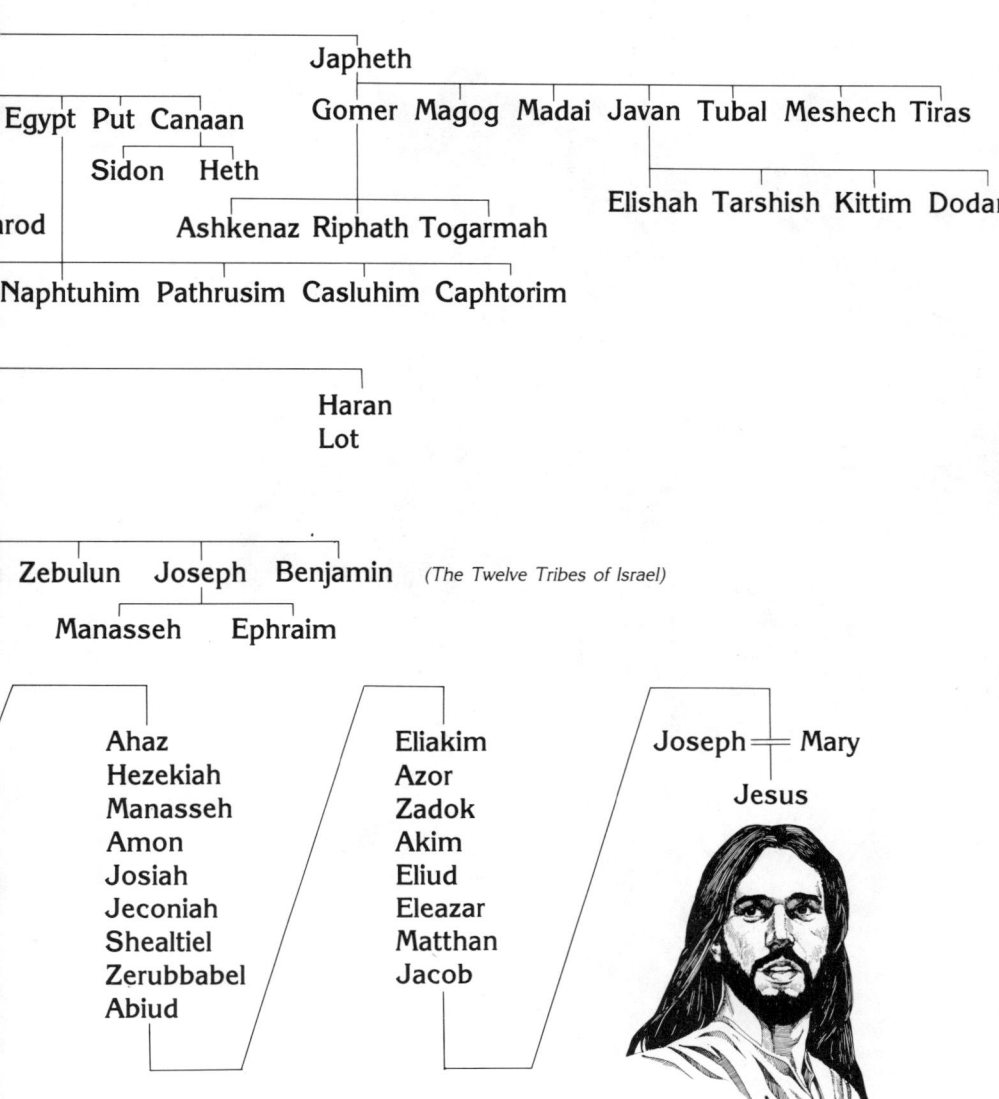

Great Prayers of the Bible

Moses' Prayer for Guidance
Exodus 33:13

I pray thee, if I have found grace in thy sight, shew me now thy way, that I may know thee, that I may find grace in thy sight: and consider that this nation is thy people. (KJV)

Moses' Prayer to See the Promised Land
Deuteronomy 3:24-25

O Lord God, thou hast begun to shew thy servant thy greatness, and thy mighty hand: for what God is there in heaven or in earth, that can do according to thy works, and according to thy might?

I pray thee, let me go over, and see the good land that is beyond Jordan, that goodly mountain, and Lebanon. (KJV)

David's Confession
II Samuel 24:10b

I have sinned greatly in that I have done: and now, I beseech thee, O Lord, take away the iniquity of thy servant; for I have done very foolishly. (KJV)

Solomon's Prayer for Wisdom
I Kings 3:7-9

"O Lord my God, you have made your servant king in place of my father David. But I am only a little child and do not know how to carry out my duties. Your servant is here among the people you have chosen, a great people, too numerous to count or number. So give your servant a discerning heart to govern your people and to distinguish between right and wrong. For who is able to govern this great people of yours?"

Praise
Psalm 9:1-2

I will praise you, O Lord, with all my heart;
   I will tell of all your wonders.
I will be glad and rejoice in you;
   I will sing praise to your name, O Most High.

For Refuge
Psalm 31:1-5

In you, O Lord, I have taken refuge;
   let me never be put to shame;
   deliver me in your righteousness.
Turn your ear to me,
   come quickly to my rescue;
be my rock of refuge,
   a strong fortress to save me.
Since you are my rock and my fortress,
   for the sake of your name lead and guide me.
Free me from the trap that is set for me,
   for you are my refuge.
Into your hands I commit my spirit;
   redeem me, O Lord, the God of truth.

For Guidance
Psalm 139:23-24

Search me, O God, and know my heart: try me, and know my thoughts:
And see if there be any wicked way in me, and lead me in the way everlasting. (KJV)

Gratitude for Deliverance
Lamentations 3:54b-58

I am cut off.
I called upon thy name, O Lord, out of the low dungeon.
Thou hast heard my voice: hide not thine ear at my breathing, at my cry.
Thou drewest near in the day that I called upon thee: thou saidst, Fear not.
O Lord, thou has pleaded the causes of my soul; thou has redeemed my life. (KJV)

Jesus at Gethsemane
Matthew 26:39

"My Father, if it is possible, may this cup be taken from me. Yet not as I will, but as you will."

Paul's Conversion Prayer
Acts 22:10

"What shall I do, Lord?"

Paul's Prayer to the Corinthians
II Corinthians 1:3-5

Praise be to the God and Father of our Lord Jesus Christ, the Father of compassion and the God of all comfort, who comforts us in all our troubles, so that we can comfort those in any trouble with the comfort we ourselves have received from God. For just as the sufferings of Christ flow over into our lives, so also through Christ our comfort overflows.

Prayer for the Coming of Jesus
Revelation 22:20b

Amen. Come, Lord Jesus.

More Great Prayers of the Bible

In the study of the following prayers, consider (1) why the person prayed, (2) what was prayed for, and (3) if the prayers were answered.

Secret Prayers

Jacob—Genesis 32:24-30
Moses—Deuteronomy 9:25-29
Samuel—I Samuel 15:11
Daniel—Daniel 6:10
Jesus—Mark 1:35
Peter—Acts 10:9
Cornelius—Acts 10:30

Short Prayers

Solomon—I Kings 3:6-9
Elijah—I Kings 17:21
Jabez—I Chronicles 4:10
Hezekiah—Isaiah 38:3
The Publican—Luke 18:13
Jesus—Luke 23:34
Stephen—Acts 7:60

Long Prayers

David—II Samuel 7:18-29
Solomon—I Kings 8:22-53
Ezra—Ezra 9:5-15
Daniel—Daniel 9:3-19
Habakkuk—Habakkuk 3:1-19
Jesus—John 17:1-26
Paul—Ephesians 3:14-21

Bible Twos

Two Destinies—Life and death, Romans 6:23

Two Masters—Righteousness and unrighteousness, Romans 6:18-22

Two Commandments—Love God and love neighbor, Matthew 22:37-40

Two Thrones—The highest heaven and the lowest heart, Isaiah 57:15

Two Sheep Dogs—"Goodness and mercy," Psalm 23:6

Two Immutable Things—Word and oath of God, Hebrews 6:17-18

Two Laws—"The law of sin and death" and "through Christ Jesus the law of the Spirit of life," Romans 8:2

Two Siftings—Israel and Peter, Amos 9:9; Luke 22:31

Two Ways to Boast—In yourself and in God, Psalm 94:4; 44:8

Two Things to Heed—What you hear and how you hear, Mark 4:24; Luke 8:18

Two Things at Which Jesus Marveled—Belief and unbelief, Matthew 8:10; Mark 6:6

Two Representative Men—The Pharisee, condemned; the publican, justified, Luke 18:9-14

Two Fools—The devil's fool and Christ's fool, Luke 12:20; I Corinthians 4:10

Two Great Evils—Forsaking God and seeking substitutes, Jeremiah 2:13

Two Adams—Head of old creation and head of the new creation, I Corinthians 15:45

Two Kinds of Peace—Peace with God, reconciliation; the peace of God, satisfaction, Romans 5:1; Philippians 4:7

Two Ways—The broad way that leads to destruction and the narrow way that leads to life eternal, Matthew 7:13-14

Two Important Prayers—"Guide me in your truth" and "let [the truth] guide me," Psalm 25:5; 43:3

Two Nameless Children—A little girl who told what she knew and a little boy who gave what he had, II Kings 5:2-4; John 6:9

Bible Threes

Three Unspeakable Possessions

Unspeakable gift, II Corinthians 9:15
Unspeakable joy, I Peter 1:8
Unspeakable experience, II Corinthians 12:2-4

Three Invitations

Come and reason, Isaiah 1:18
Come and see, John 1:46
Come and rest, Matthew 11:28

Three Falls

Demas, through the world, II Timothy 4:10
David, through the flesh, II Samuel 11:2-4
Peter, through the devil, Matthew 16:22-23

Three Perfect Things

God's work, Deuteronomy 32:4
God's way, Psalm 18:30
God's will, Romans 12:2

Three Aspects of Grace

Saved by grace, Ephesians 2:8
Stand in grace, Romans 5:2
Grow in grace, II Peter 3:18

Three Aspects of Faith

Believing in the Word of God, I John 5:9
Accepting the person of Christ, John 1:12
Committing the soul to the Lord, II Timothy 1:12

Three Aspects of Death and Sin

Death in sin, Ephesians 2:1, sinner
Death for sin, I Peter 3:18, savior
Death to sin, Romans 6:2, saint

Three Things the Lord Uses

For pruning—the knife, John 15:2
For purifying—the furnace, Malachi 3:3
For punishing—the rod, I Corinthians 4:21

Three Things We Are to Make

Straight paths for our feet, Hebrews 12:13
Our calling and election sure, II Peter 1:10
Full proof of our ministry, II Timothy 4:5

Three Things Not to Neglect

Neglect not the great salvation, Hebrews 2:3
Neglect not to stimulate believers, II Peter 1:12
Neglect not the gift that you have, I Timothy 4:14

Three Things from Which to Keep Ourselves

From idols, I John 5:21
From the world, James 1:27
From violent ways, Psalm 17:4

Three Greatest Realities

Sin has ruined all, Romans 3:23
Christ has ransomed all, I Timothy 2:6
Faith saves all, Acts 13:38-39

How to Grow

- "Pray continually." I Thessalonians 5:17

- "Rejoice in the Lord always, I will say it again: Rejoice!" Philippians 4:4

- "Add to your faith goodness; and to goodness, knowledge; and to knowledge, self-control; and to self-control, perseverance; and to perseverance, godliness; and to godliness, brotherly kindness; and to brotherly kindness, love." II Peter 1:5-7

- "You do not have, because you do not ask God." James 4:2 d

- "Do whatever he tells you." John 2:5

- "Be sure to fear the Lord and serve him faithfully with all your heart." I Samuel 12:24 a

- "Remembering the words of the Lord Jesus himself: 'It is more blessed to give than to receive.' " Acts 20:35

- "Keep yourself pure." I Timothy 5:22 b

- "Go into all the world and preach the good news to all creation." Mark 16:15

- "In all your ways acknowledge him, and he will make your paths straight." Proverbs 3:6

- "Anyone who has faith in me will do what I have been doing. He will do even greater things than these, because I am going to the Father." John 14:12

- "Endure hardship with us like a good soldier of Christ Jesus." II Timothy 2:3

Helps for Bible Reading

- When in trouble or sorrow, read John 14; Psalm 46.
- When you worry, read Matthew 6:19-34.
- When you have the blues, read Psalm 91.
- When God seems far away, read Psalm 139.
- When you want rest and peace, read Matthew 11:25-30.
- When in sickness, read James 5; Psalm 41.
- When in danger, read Luke 8:22-25; Psalm 91.
- When people fail you, read I Peter 5:7; Psalm 23.
- When lonely or fearful, read Matthew 6:25-34; 11:28-30.
- When discouraged or tempted, read I Corinthians 10:13; Isaiah 40.
- When you have sinned, read I John 1:8-9; Hebrews 7:25.
- When you forget your blessings, read Psalm 103.
- When your faith seems failing, read Hebrews 11.
- When you want courage, read II Corinthians 12:9.
- When looking for happiness, read Colossians 3:1-17.
- When leaving home for travel, read Psalm 121.
- When you grow bitter or critical, read I Corinthians 13.
- If not a Christian, read John 3:16; Matthew 10:32-33; 22:35-40; 25:31-46; Romans 10:9-13; Ephesians 2:8-9.

The Bible Story in Two-Hundred and Fifty Words

World and all things created.

Flood destroys. Noah and family saved.

God calls Abraham and covenants with him, promising him and his descendants Canaan.

Jacob is born.

Joseph is sold into Egypt, rises to prominence, and saves his father and brothers in a time of famine.

Moses becomes Israel's leader and leads the people out of Egypt. Aaron assists him. Law is given to Moses and is codified. Israel covenants with its God.

Joshua brings them into Canaan.

Gideon delivers Israel.

Israel lives under judges—Samson, Samuel. Canaan is conquered.

Monarchy is established. Saul. David. Solomon dedicates temple and covenants with God. Prophecy grows. God is called righteous, universal by Amos; loving by Hosea. Isaiah prophesies. Northern Kingdom falls in 722 B.C., Southern Kingdom in 586 B.C.

A new recodification of ancient laws about 650 B.C. Allegiance to one God, one altar, one people.

Reforms in Josiah's reign fail.

Judean kingdom falls, causing Babylonian captivity.

Ezekiel compiles priestly regulations, giving final recodifications under Ezra.

Apocalyptic idea develops. Israel, unable to conquer by sword, looks for a messiah to vindicate its aspirations.

Jesus is born, bringing a new revelation of God, and a new understanding of the nature of the Messiah and his kingdom. The Gospels record some events in his life and the story of the resurrection. At Pentecost, Jesus' Spirit comes upon his disciples.

John and Paul interpret the gospel. Hope for an immediate Second Coming of Christ is disappointed.

Churches are organized and spread among Jews and Gentiles.

Biblical Time-Line
1800 B.C.—600 B.C.

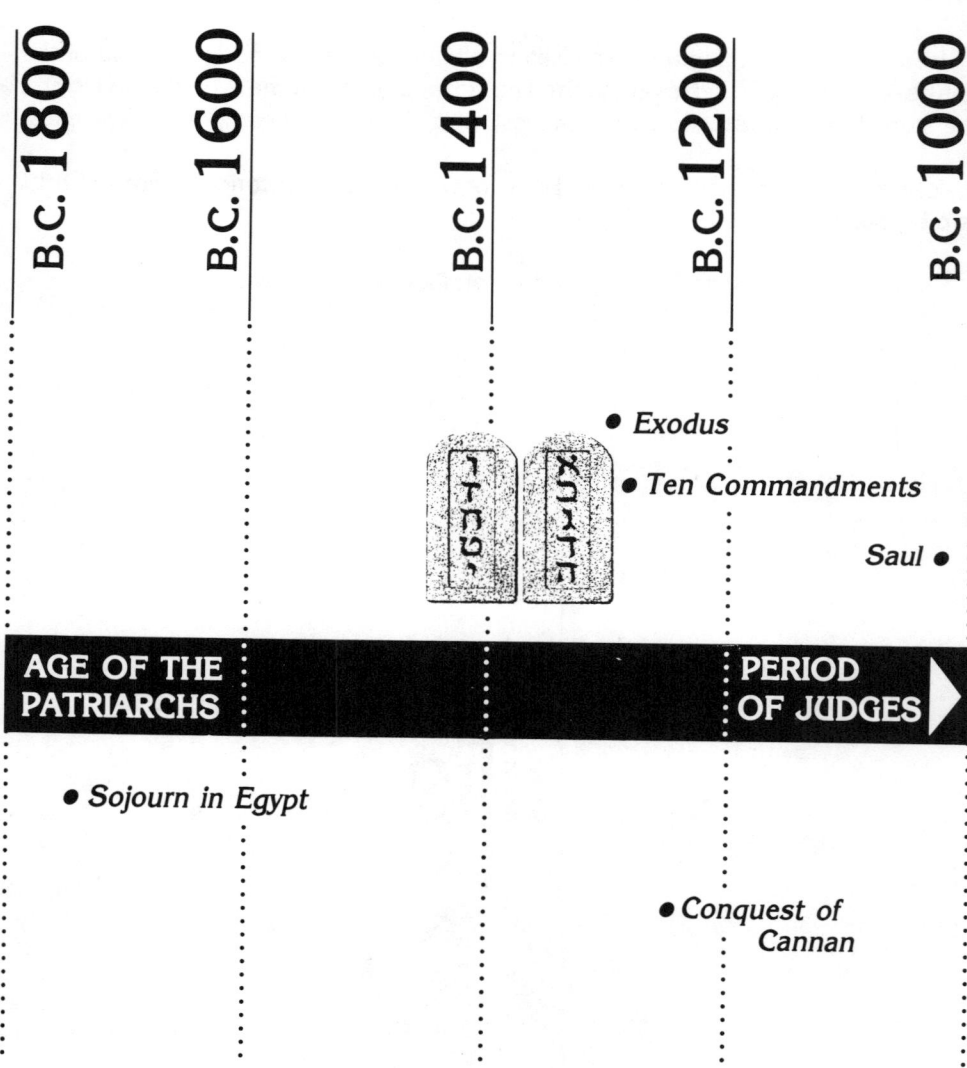

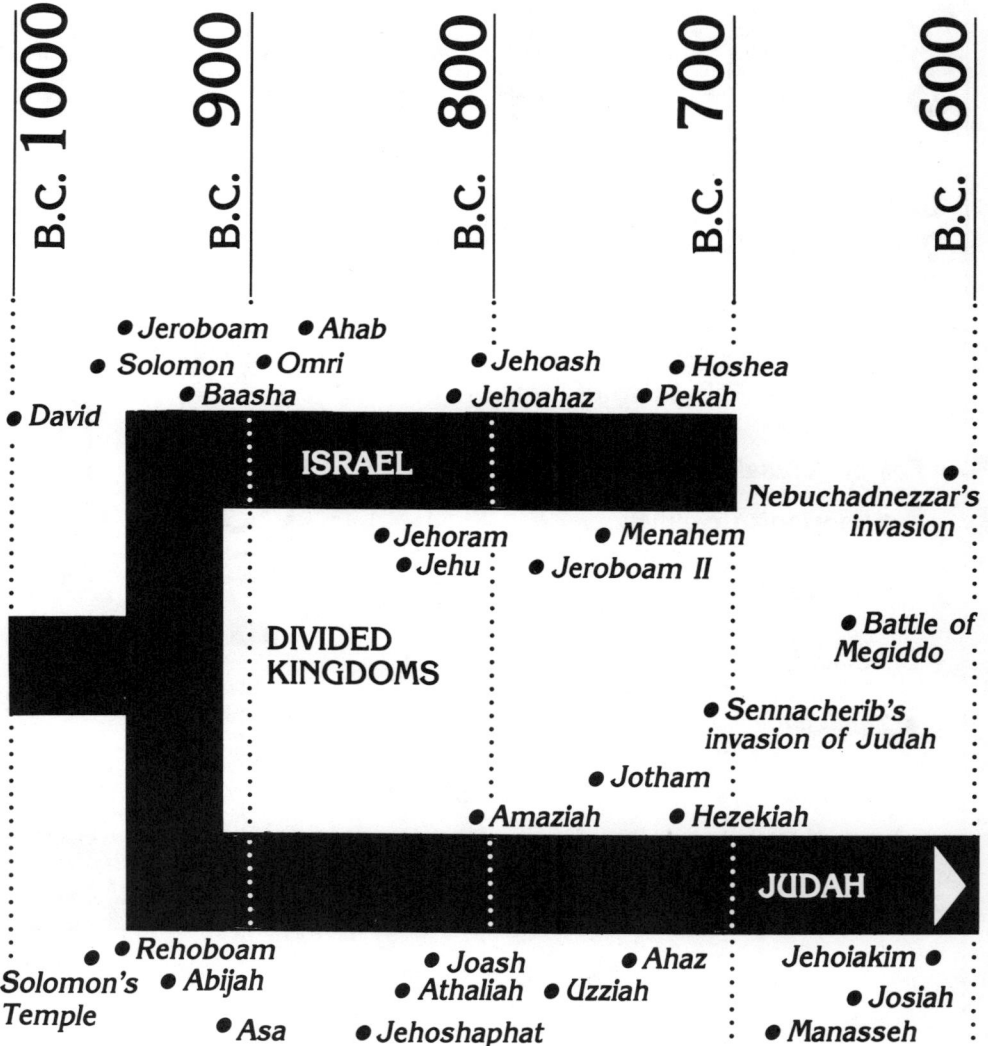

Biblical Time-Line
600 B.C.—150 B.C.

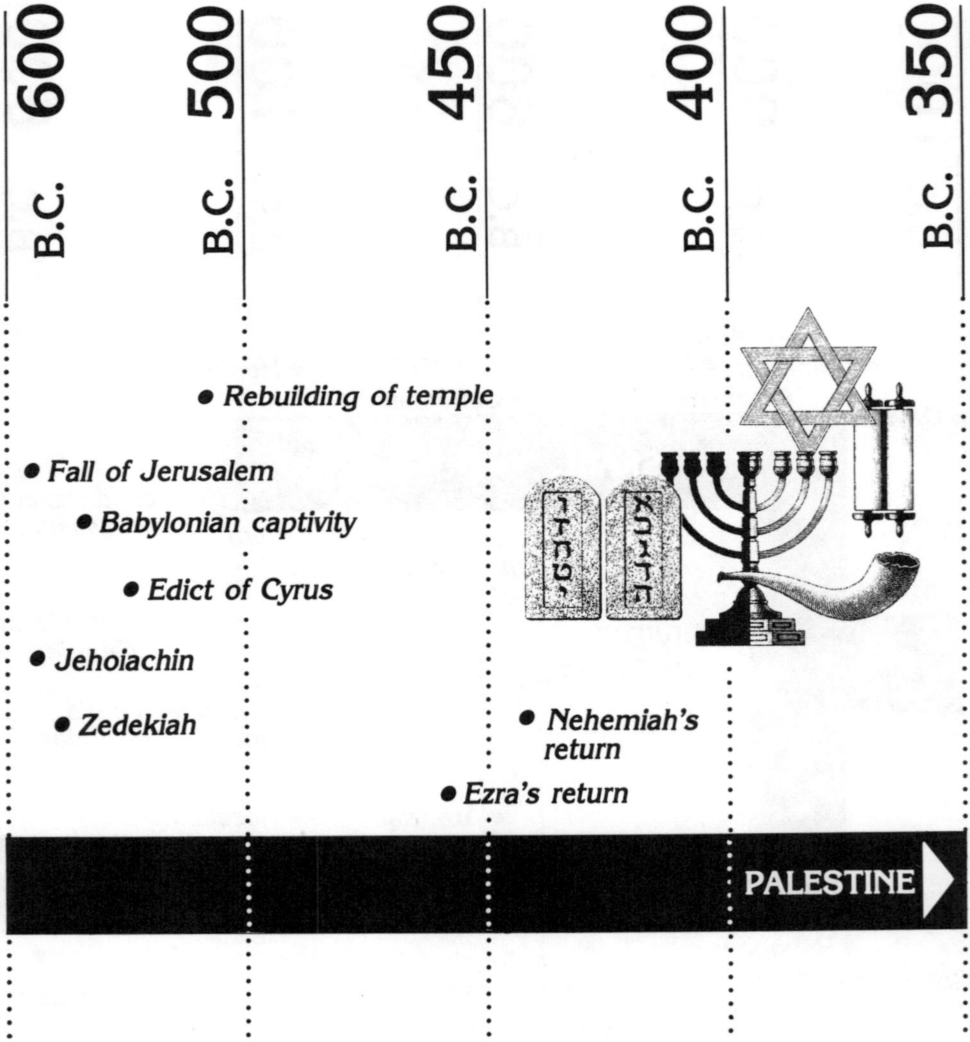

600 B.C.

500 B.C.

450 B.C.

400 B.C.

350 B.C.

- Rebuilding of temple
- Fall of Jerusalem
- Babylonian captivity
- Edict of Cyrus
- Jehoiachin
- Zedekiah
- Nehemiah's return
- Ezra's return

PALESTINE ▶

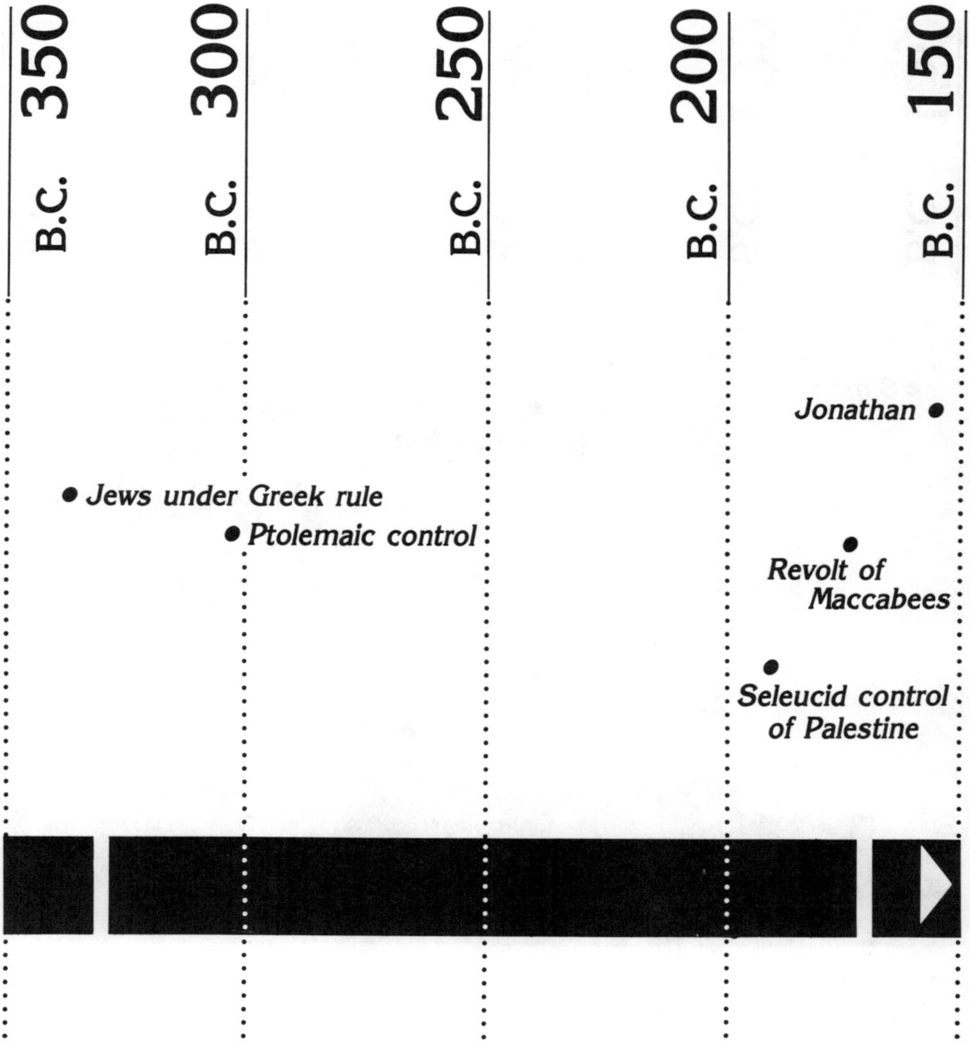

B.C. 350

B.C. 300

B.C. 250

B.C. 200

B.C. 150

- Jews under Greek rule
- Ptolemaic control

- Jonathan

- Revolt of Maccabees

- Seleucid control of Palestine

Biblical Time-Line
150 B.C.—A.D. 100

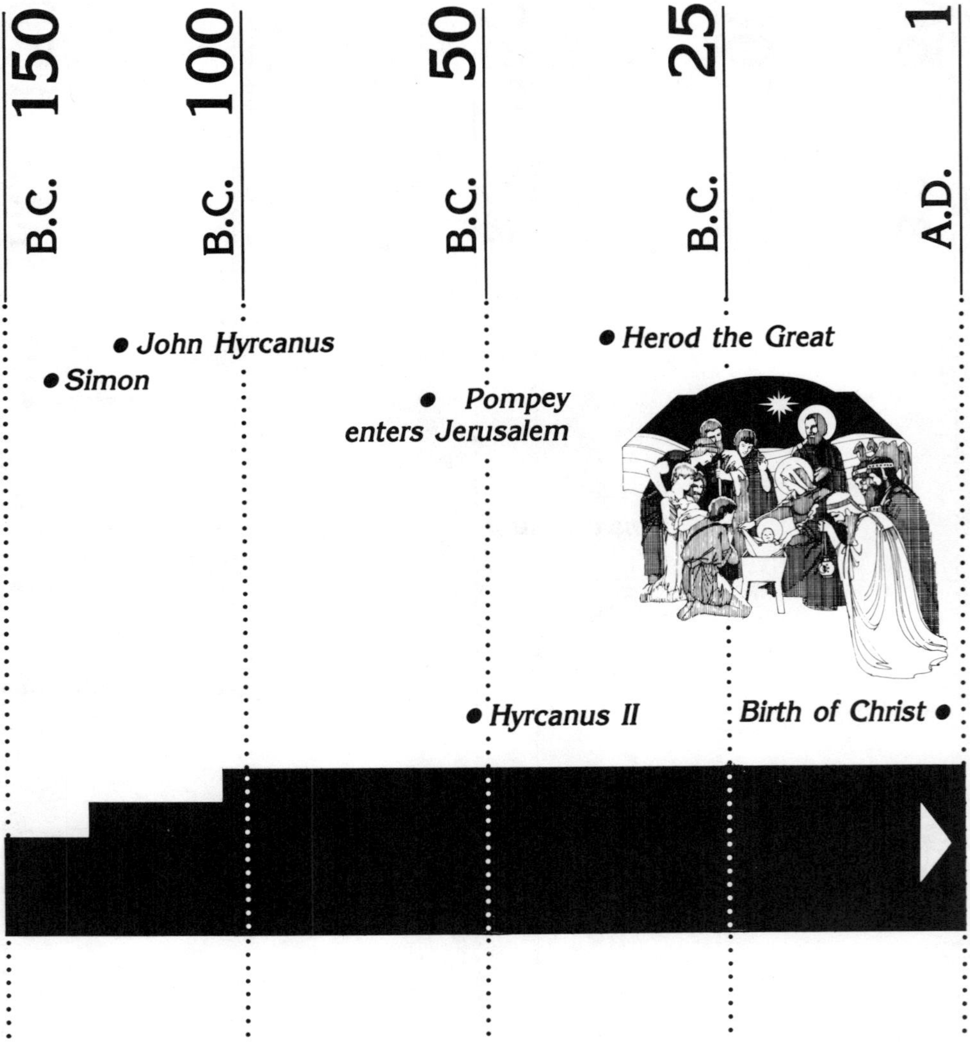

B.C. **150**
- Simon

B.C. **100**
- John Hyrcanus

B.C. **50**
- Pompey enters Jerusalem
- Hyrcanus II

B.C. **25**
- Herod the Great

A.D. **1**
- Birth of Christ

A.D. 1

A.D. 25
- Pontius Pilate
- Death of Christ
- Herod Agrippa I

A.D. 50
- Imprisonment of Paul
- Paul's missionary journeys begin

A.D. 75
- Destruction of Jerusalem
- Jewish-Roman War
- Fall of Masada

A.D. 100

My Favorite Bible Passages

My Favorite Bible Passages

My Favorite Bible Passages